Matt Miofsky

happy?
what it is and
how to find it

Leader Guide
by Maria Mayo

Abingdon Press / Nashville

happy?
what It Is and how to find it
Leader Guide

ISBN 978-1-5018-3112-6

17 18 19 20 21 22 23 24 25 26 — 10 9 8 7 6 5 4 3 2 1
MANUFACTURED IN THE UNITED STATES OF AMERICA

Contents

To the Leader

In *happy? What It Is and How to Find It*, Matt Miofsky explores the idea of lasting happiness in the biblical text and in our practical lives. He starts with an examination of Ecclesiastes and a creative look at what things do *not* contribute to happiness through the eyes of Solomon. He concludes that relationships are the essence of deep contentment, summarized in Jesus' command to love God, our neighbors, and ourselves. Miofsky then demonstrates the importance of forgiveness to relationships and lasting happiness, followed by a discussion of maintaining happiness in difficult circumstances anchored by Paul's words from prison in Philippians. Finally, he describes how lasting happiness is not simply a feeling that comes and goes, but a way of being that is consistent with living into God's plan.

In this study, Miofsky challenges readers to look beyond surface understandings of happiness and find deeper truth in Scripture and human experience. As group leader, you will lead others in a process of discernment that will help you to come together around discussions of lasting happiness and what matters most in the process of finding deep and abiding contentment. This process is dependent on the presence and guidance of the Holy Spirit. Scripture tells us that where two or three are gathered together, we can be assured of the presence of the Holy Spirit, working in and through all those gathered. As you prepare to lead, pray for that presence and expect that you will experience it.

This four-session study makes use of the following components:

- the book *happy? What It Is and How to Find It* by Matt Miofsky,
- this Leader Guide, and
- the video segments on the companion DVD.

In addition to the study book, group members will also need Bibles and either a notebook or electronic tablet for journaling. Be sure to notify those interested in the study in advance so that they may obtain copies of the book and read the Introduction and Chapter 1 before the first session.

USING THIS GUIDE WITH YOUR GROUP

Because no two groups are alike, this guide is structured to give you flexibility and choice in tailoring the sessions for your group. The basic session format is designed for a 50-minute Sunday school or other small group session, with additional options for groups wanting to explore the text in more depth. Suggested time allotments are provided only as a general guide. Select ahead of time which activities and discussion questions your group will do, for how long, and in what order—adapting the material as you wish to meet the schedule and needs of your particular group. Depending on which activities you select, special preparation may be necessary. Instructions regarding preparation are provided at the beginning of each session plan.

BASIC SESSION FORMAT

Planning the Session

Session Goals
Chapter Summary
Biblical Foundation
Special Preparation

During the Session (50 minutes)

Welcome and Opening Prayer (3 minutes)
Video (15 minutes)
Biblical Foundation (5 minutes)
Book Study (20 minutes)
Optional Activity (up to 30 minutes extra if needed)
Journaling the Week Ahead (5 minutes)
Closing Prayer (2 minutes)

After the Session

Handout: Journaling the Week Ahead

Two primary objectives undergird each group session: (1) in the session activities, participants will find help for understanding the material and connecting their beliefs with practice; (2) in Journaling the Week Ahead, group members will receive a handout with additional questions for reflection throughout the week to come.

HELPFUL HINTS

Before you get started, here are a few helpful hints to equip you for preparing, shaping, and managing the group experience:

Preparing for the Session

- Pray for the leading of the Holy Spirit as you prepare for the study. Pray for discernment for yourself and for each member of the study group.

- Before each session, read the book chapter and familiarize yourself with the content.

- Make copies of the handouts before each session to distribute at the end.

- Choose the session elements you will use during the group session, including the specific discussion questions you plan to cover. Be prepared, however, to adjust the session as group members interact and as questions arise. Prepare carefully, but allow space for the Holy Spirit to move in and through the group members and through you as facilitator.

- If you plan to use video clips or music suggestions, obtain appropriate projection equipment and test it before the session in which you plan to use it.

- Prepare the space where the group will meet so that the environment will enhance the learning process. Ideally, group members should be seated around a table or in a circle so that all can see one another. Movable chairs are best, because the group will often form pairs or small groups for discussion.

- Bring a supply of Bibles for those who forget to bring their own. Provide a variety of translations.

- For most sessions you will also need an easel with paper and markers, a whiteboard and markers, or some other means of posting group questions and responses.

Shaping the Learning Environment

- Begin and end on time.

- Establish a welcoming space. Consider the room temperature, access to amenities, hospitality, outside noise, and privacy. Consider using a small cross or candle as a focal point for times of prayer.

- Create a climate of openness, encouraging group members to participate as they feel comfortable. Some participants may be uncomfortable or embarrassed about sharing their experiences. Be on the lookout for signs of discomfort in those who may be silent, and encourage them to express their thoughts and feelings honestly. Assure the group members that passing on a question is always acceptable.

- Remember that some people will jump right in with answers and comments, while others need time to process what is being discussed.

- If you notice that some group members seem never to be able to enter the conversation, ask them if they have thoughts to share. Give everyone a chance to talk, but keep the conversation moving. Moderate to prevent a few individuals from doing all the talking.

- Make use of the exercises that invite sharing in pairs. Those who are reluctant to speak out in a group setting may be more comfortable sharing one-on-one and reporting back to the group. This can often be an effective means of helping people grow more comfortable sharing in the larger setting. It also helps to avoid the dominance of the group by one or two participants (including you!).

- If no one answers at first during discussions, do not be afraid of silence. Help the group become comfortable with waiting. If no one responds, try reframing the language of the question. If no responses are forthcoming, venture an answer yourself and ask for comments.

- Model openness as you share with the group. Group members will follow your example. If you limit your sharing to a surface level, others will follow suit.

- Encourage multiple answers or responses before moving on to the next discussion point.

- Ask "Why?" or "Why do you believe that?" or "Can you say more about that?" to help continue a discussion and give it greater depth.

- Affirm others' responses with comments such as "great" or "thanks" or "good insight"—especially if it's the first time someone has spoken during the group session.

- Monitor your own contributions. If you are doing most of the talking, back off so that you do not train the group to listen rather than speak up.

- Remember that you do not have all the answers. Your job is to keep the discussion going and encourage participation.

Managing the Session

- Honor the time schedule. If a session is running longer than expected, get consensus from the group before continuing beyond the agreed-upon ending time.

- When someone arrives late or *must* leave early, pause the session *briefly* to welcome them or bid them farewell. Changes in the makeup of the group change the dynamics of the discussion and need to be acknowledged. Every group member is important to the entire group.

- Involve group members in various aspects of the group session, such as saying prayers or reading the Scripture.

- As always in discussions that may involve personal sharing, confidentiality is essential. Group members should never pass along stories that have been shared in the group. Remind the group members at each session: confidentiality is crucial to the success of this study.

Session 1

Nothing Will Make You Happy

Session 1

Nothing Will Make You Happy

PLANNING THE SESSION

Session Goals

As a result of conversations and activities connected with this session, group members should begin to:

- consider the definition and meaning of lasting happiness;
- understand through an exploration of Ecclesiastes how work, material possessions and accomplishments, and the pursuit of pleasure do not lead to lasting happiness; and
- explore how relationships provide the surest basis for lasting happiness.

Chapter Summary

In Chapter 1, Matt Miofsky surveys the Book of Ecclesiastes in an exploration of the search for meaning and happiness. In this Scripture, Solomon finds that work, material possessions and accomplishments, and the pursuit of pleasure do not lead to lasting happiness. In fact, initially it appears that nothing at all leads to happiness; everything is pointless. For Solomon, life is futile, repetitive, and fleeting.

We place great value on our work, our accomplishments, and our pleasurable pursuits. While none of these leads to happiness, Solomon does recognize the value of relationships and sticking together. Miofsky uses Solomon's observation to show that the true source of lasting happiness comes from nurturing the relationships described in Jesus' love commandment: relationship with God, neighbor, and self. Other pursuits may contribute to happiness in our lives, but only when we strengthen these relationships will we find deep and abiding happiness.

Biblical Foundation

What do people gain from all the hard work
that they work so hard at under the sun?
A generation goes, and a generation comes,
but the earth remains as it always has.
The sun rises, the sun sets;
it returns panting to the place where it dawns.
The wind blows to the south,
goes around to the north;
around and around blows the wind;
the wind returns to its rounds again.

16

All streams flow to the sea,
*   but the sea is never full;*
*   to the place where the rivers flow,*
*   there they continue to flow.*
All words are tiring;
*   no one is able to speak.*
*   The eye isn't satisfied with seeing,*
*   neither is the ear filled up by hearing.*
Whatever has happened—that's what will happen again;
*   whatever has occurred—that's what will occur again.*

There's nothing new under the sun....

When I observed all that happens under the sun, I
realized that everything is pointless, a chasing after wind.

                                        (Ecclesiastes 1:3-9, 14)

Two are better than one because they have a good return
for their hard work. If either should fall, one can pick
up the other. But how miserable are those who fall and
don't have a companion to help them up! Also, if two lie
down together, they can stay warm. But how can anyone
stay warm alone? Also, one can be overpowered, but two
together can put up resistance. A three-ply cord doesn't
easily snap.

                                        (Ecclesiastes 4:9-12)

"You must love the Lord your God with all your heart,
with all your being, *and with all your mind. This is the*
first and greatest commandment. And the second is like
it: You must love your neighbor as you love yourself."

                                        (Matthew 22:37-39)

17

Special Preparation

- Provide writing paper and pens for those who may need them. Also have Bibles available for those who do not bring one.

- Make sure all participants have a copy of the book *happy? What It Is and How to Find It.* Invite them to read the introduction and Chapter 1 in advance of the first session.

- Have available large sheets of blank paper to attach to the wall or a large whiteboard and markers for group activity.

- Bring index cards to distribute for group activity.

- Make copies of Session 1 Handout for the group.

- As leader, go over the session in advance and select or adapt the activities you think will work best for your group in the time allotted. Consider your own responses to questions you will pose to the group.

- Make name tags available if desired.

DURING THE SESSION

Welcome and Opening Prayer (3 minutes)

As participants arrive, welcome them to the study and invite them to make use of one of the available Bibles, if they did not bring one. Offer the following prayer, pray one of your own, or invite a group member to pray.

Gracious and loving God, as we begin this study, open us to your presence and fill us—our time, our conversations, our reflections, our doubts, and our fears—with the joy of exploration and the wisdom of your love. We gather together in Jesus' name. Amen.

Video (15 minutes)

Play the video for Session 1. In this segment, Matt Miofsky explores the Book of Ecclesiastes to find answers about what brings meaning and happiness to human lives.

Choose from the following for a brief discussion:

- Do you agree that work, material possessions and accomplishments, and the pursuit of pleasure will not lead to lasting happiness? Why or why not? In what ways might those aspects of life enrich relationships and contribute to happiness?

- Ecclesiastes 5:11 reads, "When good things flow, so do those who consume them." How do you interpret this statement? What meaning does Miofsky offer? How does this verse speak to lasting happiness?

- Miofsky describes Ecclesiastes as "an Eeyore-type book." What do you think he means by this? Do you agree?

- He describes the endless accumulation of possessions as creating a "hamster wheel effect." What does he mean by this metaphor? How have you seen this happen in your own lives?

Biblical Foundation (5 minutes)

Chapter 1 cites Ecclesiastes 1:3-8 as interpreted in the CEB. Read the passage aloud and choose from the following for discussion:

- How does this passage point to futility in the cycles of life and nature? Must such cycles always lead to despair as they do for Solomon?
- How might the passage be a comfort, or even a source of happiness, to some readers?
- The phrase "under the sun" appears twenty times in Ecclesiastes. What do you think Solomon is getting at with these words? Consider these verses:
- "What do people gain from all the hard work that they work so hard at under the sun?" (1:3)
- "There's nothing new under the sun." (1:9)
- "When I observed all that happens under the sun, I realized that everything is pointless, a chasing after wind." (1:14)
- Solomon was searching for happiness and meaning in life, but here he seems to feel that such a search is futile. Do you agree or disagree?

Book Study (20 minutes)

Chapter 1 begins with a discussion of a scientific study on happiness, and goes on to imagine the Book of Ecclesiastes as a similar study on what makes for lasting happiness. Solomon explores several hypotheses about what will lead to happiness: work, material possessions and accomplishments, and the pursuit of pleasure.

Explore the chapter's content together with the following exercises:

Chasing Happiness

On a large piece of paper or whiteboard at the front of the room, write "Lasting Happiness" at the top of one column, and "Contributors to Happiness" at the top of a second column. Invite the class to consider the following questions and write their responses on the paper or whiteboard. Under "Lasting Happiness," list definitions of lasting happiness. Under "Contributors to Happiness," list aspects of life that might contribute to lasting happiness.

- How do you define lasting happiness? What are its key elements?
- What aspects of life contribute to lasting happiness?
- Might work, material possessions and accomplishments, and pleasurable pursuits contribute to lasting happiness in some way?

Once you've filled out both columns, ask the class to consider the answers and compare them with the author's definition. Did the class reach the same conclusion as the author? Open the floor for deeper sharing about experiences in pursuing lasting happiness. What worked and what didn't?

The Facebook Effect

Miofsky describes the Facebook Effect as follows: "Researchers have shown pretty convincingly that Facebook fuels our sense of competition with one another, because we tend to post great things. . . . Every time we see those things on someone else's Facebook page, they make us feel that we need to catch up."

Give each person a notecard and pen. Have the group think back on the last Facebook post they viewed that made them feel inadequate or competitive. On the notecard, write what you remember from the post and brainstorm why it might have struck a chord with you.

21

After a few minutes, ask for volunteers to share their reflections (without using names). Consider the following questions for discussion:

- How did you feel when you saw this post? What was the first thought to cross your mind?

- If you felt inadequate or competitive, what did you do about feeling that way?

- In what ways can we conduct our lives on social media to sustain and nurture our relationships rather than threaten our self-esteem?

Optional Activity (up to 30 minutes extra)

Thinking About Relationships

Post the following questions on paper or whiteboard:

- In what ways has your reliance on work, material possessions and accomplishments, and the pursuit of pleasure led you away from happiness in your life instead of toward it?

- How does Jesus' love commandment provide a new direction for happiness? How might relationships be the answer? Read aloud:

"You must love the Lord your God with all your heart, with all your being, *and with all your mind. This is the first and greatest commandment. And the second is like it:* You must love your neighbor as you love yourself."

(*Matthew 22:37-39*)

Invite participants into conversation in small groups of three or four. The questions are designed to help people think about how their relationships with God, others, and themselves have resulted in a deep sense of happiness in their lives. This process helps us learn how to tell our stories and how to actively listen to and learn from the stories of others.

Give the small groups 15 minutes to share their responses with one another. Remind them that as each person shares, the task of the listeners is to attend to and receive the story in attentive silence. Remind them that each person should have the opportunity to share, and that persons may choose not to share.

At the end of the 15 minutes of small group time, invite the groups back together. Ask them to share insights gained from hearing one another's stories and from sharing their own. How has their understanding of happiness changed over time? What does the variety of perspectives on happiness tell us about our relationships with God, ourselves, and one another?

Journaling the Week Ahead (5 minutes)

At this point in the session, distribute Session 1 Handout with journal prompts and additional questions. Explain to the class that the handout is for their personal use in the week ahead to continue to explore the issues raised in class.

Closing Prayer (2 minutes)

God of eternal love, fill us with your power as we leave this place, so that all we have shared and learned here helps us to be more faithful disciples. As your church in and for the world, we pray in the name of Jesus the Christ. Amen.

JOURNALING THE WEEK AHEAD

Read this quotation from Chapter 1 of the book:

> If you've invested everything you have in your job,
> if it has been your primary driver of meaning,
> purpose, and contentment and then it ends, what
> happens? Solomon found that when work goes away
> so will your happiness.

Is it possible to challenge Solomon on this understanding of the
relationship between work and happiness?

_____

_____

_____

_____

_____

_____

_____

The author also posits that material possessions and accomplishments are equally lacking.

> Researchers have shown pretty convincingly that
> Facebook fuels our sense of competition with one
> another, because we tend to post great things.... Every
> time we see those things on someone else's Facebook
> page, they make us feel that we need to catch up.

Is it possible to challenge the author and make the case that social media might also be a contributor to lasting happiness?

_____

_____

_____

_____

_____

_____

Based on the author's conclusion that relationships are the key to lasting happiness, what might it mean to lose a relationship? What is the impact of a devastating breakup, the loss of an important friendship, or the death of a loved one on the kind of lasting happiness embodied in the love commandment?

_____

_____

_____

_____

_____

_____

Session 2

The Art of Forgiveness

The Art of Forgiveness

PLANNING THE SESSION

Session Goals

As a result of conversations and activities connected with this session, group members should begin to:

- understand the relationship between forgiveness and lasting happiness;

- learn the nature of God's forgiveness and its relationship to human forgiveness; and

- explore how forgiveness can heal relationships, both with others and ourselves.

Chapter Summary

In Chapter 2, Matt Miofsky explores the relationship between forgiveness and lasting happiness. God's forgiveness has several features: it can include judgment and anger, it is aimed at reconciliation and restoration, and it is costly. Human forgiveness is often complicated and confusing, and may often be blocked by anger and fear. Beyond these obstacles, however, forgiveness of others and forgiveness of the self can contribute to healthier relationships and greater happiness. Willingness to forgive helps us change our perspective on others, cultivate compassion, and stop the cycle of anger and revenge. Repairing relationships helps transform anger into grace and love. As Miofsky observes, "It's really hard to be happy if you're always mad."

Biblical Foundation

Then Peter said to Jesus, "Lord, how many times should I forgive my brother or sister who sins against me? Should I forgive as many as seven times?"

Jesus said, "Not just seven times, but rather as many as seventy-seven times."

(Matthew 18:21-22)

God was reconciling the world to himself through Christ, by not counting people's sins against them. He has trusted us with this message of reconciliation.

(2 Corinthians 5:19)

*Put away from you all bitterness and wrath and anger
and wrangling and slander, together with all malice,
and be kind to one another, tenderhearted, forgiving one
another, as God in Christ has forgiven you.*

(Ephesians 4:31-32 NRSV)

*Know this, my dear brothers and sisters: everyone should
be quick to listen, slow to speak, and slow to grow angry.
This is because an angry person doesn't produce God's
righteousness.*

(James 1:19-20)

Special Preparation

- Provide writing paper and pens for those who may need them. Also have Bibles available for those who do not bring one.

- Invite participants to read Chapter 2 in advance of the session.

- Have available large sheets of blank paper or a whiteboard for group activity.

- Make copies of Session 2 Handout for the group.

- As leader, you'll want to go over the session in advance and select or adapt the activities you think will work best for your group in the time allotted. Consider your own responses to questions you will pose to the group.

- Make name tags available if desired.

DURING THE SESSION

Welcome and Opening Prayer (3 minutes)

As participants arrive, welcome them to the study and invite them to make use of one of the available Bibles, if they did not bring one. Offer the following prayer, pray one of your own, or invite a group member to pray.

Joyous and giving God, we gather to learn, share, laugh, and grow in faith and joy. Accompany us on the journey. Amen.

Video (15 minutes)

Play the video for Session 2. The segment suggests that forgiveness is key to our relationship with God, with ourselves, and with others. Our forgiveness of one another is inextricably related to God's forgiveness of us.

Choose from the following for a brief discussion:

- What does Miofsky identify as a "forgiving lifestyle"? How can a change of perspective toward others improve relationships and open the way for forgiveness?

- In 2 Corinthians 5:17 we read, "If anyone is in Christ, that person is part of the new creation. The old things have gone away, and look, new things have arrived!" How does this verse relate to forgiveness? In what way does forgiveness give way to a new creation?

Biblical Foundation (5 minutes)

Read aloud Matthew 18:21-22 and discuss:

- What does the passage teach about the bounds of human forgiveness?
- In what circumstances would it be difficult for you to follow Jesus' instruction? Why?
- How is Christ's message of reconciliation illustrated in the "seventy-seven times" verses? How is human forgiveness meant to imitate Christ's forgiveness?
- What does the passage from James teach about the place of anger? Why doesn't an angry person reflect God's righteousness? Does God ever get angry?

Book Study (20 minutes)

Chapter 2 begins with the contention that forgiveness is essential for good relationships, and good relationships are the key to lasting happiness. Explore the chapter content together with the following exercises:

Defining Forgiveness

The chapter offers a number of explanations of forgiveness and descriptions of its benefits. Divide the group into three small groups and give each a large piece of paper and marker along with some extra paper for writing down responses. Have each group explore the following questions and then come up with a one-sentence definition for forgiveness beginning with "Forgiveness is…" Be sure to capture the group's ideas as you work toward a definition.

- What does the act of forgiveness include? What does it not include?

- What is the purpose of forgiveness?

- Who reaps the benefits of forgiveness, the forgiver or the forgiven?

- Are Christians always required to forgive? Explain your response.

- How is forgiveness an essential ingredient to lasting happiness?

Ask each group to choose a reporter. When the groups have completed their work, invite the reporter from each group to post their definition on the wall and explain how they arrived at their conclusion.

Forgiveness Role Play

Ask two female or two male volunteers to sit in chairs at the front of the room. Explain to the group that they will play the roles of good friends who have become estranged. Several weeks ago, one of the friends confided that her/his marriage was in serious trouble and her/his spouse had had an affair. The person implored the friend to keep this a secret. However, the friend later gossiped about the news, and soon the entire church community knew about it and began taking sides. Now the friend who betrayed the confidence is remorseful and wants to be forgiven. The friend asked to meet for coffee to talk about it. Have the two volunteers play out this meeting in front of the group. The conversation should last about five minutes, and it may or may not end with an expression of forgiveness.

Once the role play is completed, thank the volunteers and ask them to rejoin the group. Next, ask the group to consider the following questions together:

- What steps did the friends go through in confronting the topic of forgiveness? Do you think any steps were missing?

- What would be compelling arguments for forgiveness in this situation?

- If the interaction ended with forgiveness, what were the benefits? What were the risks?

- What effect does forgiveness have on our relationships with one another? with God?

- Some say that forgiveness is the absence of anger. Would that be true in this case?

- Would you have forgiven your friend? Why or why not?

Optional Activity (up to 30 minutes extra)

Forgiveness and Anger

God isn't about anger or punishment. Yet, just after Jesus instructs his followers to forgive "seventy-seven times," he offers the following parable. Read the parable aloud and consider the questions together as a group.

> *"Therefore, the kingdom of heaven is like a king who wanted to settle accounts with his servants. When he began to settle accounts, they brought to him a servant who owed him ten thousand bags of gold. Because the servant didn't have enough to pay it back, the master*

ordered that he should be sold, along with his wife and children and everything he had, and that the proceeds should be used as payment. But the servant fell down, kneeled before him, and said, 'Please, be patient with me, and I'll pay you back.' The master had compassion on that servant, released him, and forgave the loan.

"*When that servant went out, he found one of his fellow servants who owed him one hundred coins. He grabbed him around the throat and said, 'Pay me back what you owe me.'*

"*Then his fellow servant fell down and begged him, 'Be patient with me, and I'll pay you back.' But he refused. Instead, he threw him into prison until he paid back his debt.*

"*When his fellow servants saw what happened, they were deeply offended. They came and told their master all that happened. His master called the first servant and said, 'You wicked servant! I forgave you all that debt because you appealed to me. Shouldn't you also have mercy on your fellow servant, just as I had mercy on you?' His master was furious and handed him over to the guard responsible for punishing prisoners, until he had paid the whole debt.*

"*My heavenly Father will also do the same to you if you don't forgive your brother or sister from your heart.*"

(Matthew 18:23-35)

In this parable, the king who represents God *does* appear angry and ready to punish. Why? What happens to change his mind? What do you think is the meaning of this parable? How does it fit with the instruction to forgive "seventy-seven times"? Are there acts that simply cannot be forgiven by God? by human beings? What would you include on that list?

Colossians 3:13 reads, "Be tolerant with each other and, if someone has a complaint against anyone, forgive each other. As the Lord forgave you, so also forgive each other." How is God's forgiveness different from human forgiveness? How is it similar? What does it mean to model our forgiveness of each other after God's forgiveness of us?

Journaling the Week Ahead (5 minutes)

At this point in the session, distribute Session 2 Handout with journal prompts and additional questions. Explain to the class that the handout is for their personal use in the week ahead to continue to explore the issues raised in class.

Closing Prayer (2 minutes)

God of transformation, God of joy, walk with us this week as we stretch to learn new skills in the ways we communicate and share with others. Amen.

JOURNALING THE WEEK AHEAD

Read these words from Chapter 2:

> If we ever want lasting happiness or a deep sense of joy and peace, then we have to figure out how to achieve good relationships. But good relationships— with God, with ourselves, and with others—all hinge on our ability to practice one simple art. It's the art of forgiveness.

Do you agree with this statement? How does forgiveness affect each of these relationships—with God, with ourselves, and with others?

_____

_____

_____

_____

How is the parable of the prodigal son an example of forgiveness? How does the father's reaction to the son mirror God's reactions to us? Can we always expect to be forgiven by God no matter what we do?

_____

_____

_____

_____

Consider this quotation: "There is a cost to forgiving, but the cost to us and the world for not forgiving is even higher, because through forgiveness comes healing." How is forgiveness costly to human beings? What does it cost in everyday life? Is it always worth it?

_____

_____

_____

_____

_____

_____

Miofsky contends, "Really, the whole purpose of Jesus' ministry... was this: to let us know we are forgiven and to change our relationship with God." Explain how forgiveness was the whole purpose of Jesus' ministry. What examples of Jesus' teaching deliver this message?

_____

_____

_____

_____

_____

_____

_____

_____

Session 3

Beyond
Circumstances

Session 3

Beyond Circumstances

PLANNING THE SESSION

Session Goals

As a result of conversations and activities connected with this session, group members should begin to:

- learn four keys to true contentment as presented in Scripture,

- explore the process of changing perspective, and

- discern how to find happiness regardless of circumstances.

Chapter Summary

The author opens with Scripture from Philippians in which Paul writes from prison about his ability to be happy in spite of his difficult circumstances. One characteristic of lasting happiness is being able to find joy and contentment in spite of your circumstances. Miofsky identifies four keys to lasting happiness: living in the present, changing your perspective, being grateful, and letting go of control. He concludes that shifting circumstances are easier to deal with when happiness is rooted in God. Finding contentment in God, he writes, prevents happiness from coming and going as times change.

Biblical Foundation

Be glad in the Lord always! Again I say, be glad! Let your gentleness show in your treatment of all people. The Lord is near. Don't be anxious about anything; rather, bring up all your requests to God in your prayers and petitions, along with giving thanks. Then the peace of God that exceeds all understanding will keep your hearts and minds safe in Christ Jesus. . . .

I'm not saying this because I need anything, for I have learned how to be content in any circumstance. I know the experience of being in need and of having more than enough; I have learned the secret to being content in any and every circumstance, whether full or hungry or whether having plenty or being poor. I can endure all these things through the power of the one who gives me strength.

(Philippians 4:4-7, 11-13)

"Stop worrying about tomorrow, because tomorrow will worry about itself. Each day has enough trouble of its own."

(Matthew 6:34)

Special Preparation

- Provide writing paper and pens for those who may need them. Also have Bibles available for those who do not bring one.

- Invite participants to read Chapter 3 in advance of the session and remind them to bring their journals with them.

- Have available large sheets of blank paper (newsprint) or construction paper and colored markers for group activity.

- Make copies of Session 3 Handout for the group.

- As leader, go over the session in advance and select or adapt the activities you think will work best for your group in the time allotted. Consider your own responses to questions you will pose to the group.

- Make name tags available if desired.

DURING THE SESSION

Welcome and Opening Prayer (3 minutes)

As participants arrive, welcome them to the study and invite them to make use of one of the available Bibles, if they did not bring one. Offer the following prayer, pray one of your own, or invite a group member to pray.

God of wisdom and discernment, teach us to link our passion with belief, our belief with action, and our action with you. Amen.

Video (15 minutes)

Play the video for Session 3. The segment suggests that lasting happiness is less a result of our circumstances and more a function of our perspective on those circumstances. Miofsky proposes that living in the present and changing your perspective, along with remembering to feel gratitude and letting go of control, can lead to true contentment more than any change in external circumstances.

Choose from the following for a brief discussion:

- Miofsky emphasizes that the kind of happiness he's talking about is not simply an emotion or feeling, but rather a "scriptural idea." What is the promise of Scripture he is talking about? How is the ability to cultivate contentment different from seeking happiness?

- He observes, "Sometimes perspective matters more to our happiness than the circumstances themselves." Do you agree? Why or why not?

Biblical Foundation (5 minutes)

The author defines *contentment* as "an abiding sense of peace, hope, [and] joy." The promise of Scripture, he writes, is that "we can find this deep level of contentment independent of circumstances."

Read aloud the biblical passage for this session, Philippians 4:11-13, which is part of Paul's message of thanks to the Philippians for supporting his mission.

- How does this passage connect with the author's words about finding contentment in every circumstance?

- Paul writes, "I have learned the secret to being content in any and every circumstance, whether full or hungry or whether having plenty or being poor. I can endure all these things through the power of the one who gives me strength." (4:12-13) What is the secret? Do you find that you can be content in every circumstance through the power of God?

Book Study (20 minutes)

Explore the content of Chapter 3 together with the following exercises:

A Change in Perspective

Photocopy and distribute the image included at the end of this session plan. Ask the class to identify the animal in the picture. Some may say rabbit; others may say duck. Challenge the class to shift perspective and try to see the other animal. Miofsky writes, "When we get a new perspective, sometimes we can see the same circumstance in an entirely new way." What can we learn from the rabbit/duck exercise about shifting perspectives? What events in your life have required a change in perspective, and how did you accomplish that? How does Paul shift his perspective when he is in prison? What is the outcome for Paul?

Gratitude Journal

Gratitude is an important part of cultivating contentment. Some keep a "gratitude journal" in which they daily write down a few things they are grateful for. This can often bring a change in perspective by shifting the focus away from things that are troubling and concentrating instead on things that bring happiness or joy, like good health, family, a steady job, or close friendships.

Give each member of the group a piece of paper and a pen. Have them make a short list of things they are grateful for. When they are finished, allow willing members to share all or part of their lists. Reflect on the following questions:

- How did completing this exercise help you focus less on things that are bothering you?
- What did you realize as you thought about what you were truly grateful for?
- Did you experience a change in perspective on what things are important?
- Do you think you might employ a gratitude journal as a daily discipline? Why or why not?

Optional Activity (up to 30 minutes extra)

Cultivating Contentment

The author proposes four keys to cultivating contentment. Divide the group into four teams. Post a large sheet of paper on the wall for each team. Assign each team one of the four keys: living in the present, changing your perspective, experiencing gratitude, and letting go of control. Have each team brainstorm both the meaning and practical applications of their key.

After five minutes, have the teams come back together as one group. Ask a reporter from each team to present their findings to the group. Discuss the following questions:

- How do these keys contribute to lasting happiness?

- How do these keys come together to build the kind of lasting happiness described by Paul in Philippians?

- Was it difficult to come up with a description or practical application of your key?

- Do you agree that these are the basic keys to lasting happiness? What would you add or take away?

- Is there one of these keys on which you especially need to focus on?

Journaling the Week Ahead (5 minutes)

At this point in the session, distribute Session 3 Handout with journal prompts and additional questions. Explain to the class that the handout is for their personal use in the week ahead to continue to explore the issues raised in class.

Closing Prayer (2 minutes)

God, grant me the serenity to accept the things I cannot change, the courage to change the things I can, and the wisdom to know the difference. Amen.

JOURNALING THE WEEK AHEAD

What is the difference between the "feeling" of happiness and the deep level of contentment, peace, and joy described by the author? Does the emotional aspect of happiness have a place in that contentment? What is its value to us?

_____

_____

_____

_____

_____

_____

The author writes, "Two of the greatest obstacles to lasting happiness are regrets about the past and anxiety about the future." How does focusing on the present moment contribute to lasting happiness? How does Paul's response to being in prison illustrate this point?

_____

_____

_____

_____

_____

Finish the following sentence: "I would be happy if I had _____."
How can a change in perspective from what we don't have to what
we do have contribute to happiness? How do you maintain joy when
you are having a bad day, or week, or year?

_____

_____

_____

_____

_____

Read these words from Chapter 3:

> What helps Paul cultivate contentment and happiness
> in his life, even when in prison, is that he trusts that
> God is in control. He believes with all his heart that
> God is working for his welfare and not his harm, and
> is creating a future with hope.

How difficult is it to have faith like Paul's? Why is it so hard for us
to let go of control and trust that God is looking out for us?

_____

_____

_____

_____

_____

_____

"A CHANGE IN PERSPECTIVE"
ILLUSTRATION

Session 4

A Way of Being

Session 4

A Way of Being

PLANNING THE SESSION

Session Goals

As a result of conversations and activities connected with this session, group members should begin to:

- explore the relationship between lasting happiness and God's desire for us,

- learn how generosity and selfless acts contribute to deep contentment, and

- understand how following the life and words of Jesus leads to a sense of peace and joy.

55

Chapter Summary

The author describes how most contemporary literature on happiness recommends a focus on the self. Turning toward what God wants for us rather than what we want for ourselves is one key to lasting happiness. Another comes from shifting the focus away from the self and onto others through acts of generosity and caring. Through such acts we live into the life God desires for us, and thus into lasting happiness. Through generosity we gain a new perspective, we find ourselves to be used and useful, and we are directed to the things that matter most.

Biblical Foundation

Jesus said to everyone, "All who want to come after me must say no to themselves, take up their cross daily, and follow me. All who want to save their lives will lose them. But all who lose their lives because of me will save them."

(Luke 9:23-24)

"The thief enters only to steal, kill, and destroy. I came so that they could have life—indeed, so that they could live life to the fullest."

(John 10:10)

My plans aren't your plans,
nor are your ways my ways, says the LORD.
Just as the heavens are higher than the earth,
so are my ways higher than your ways,
and my plans than your plans.

(Isaiah 55:8-9)

Special Preparation

- Provide writing paper and pens for those who may need them. Also have Bibles available for those who do not bring one.

- Invite participants to read Chapter 4 in advance of the session and remind them to bring their journals with them.

- Have available large sheets of blank paper (newsprint) or construction paper and colored markers for group activity.

- Make copies of Session 4 Handout for the group.

- As leader, you'll want to go over the session in advance and select or adapt the activities you think will work best for your group in the time allotted. Consider your own responses to questions you will pose to the group.

- Make name tags available if desired.

DURING THE SESSION

Welcome and Opening Prayer (3 minutes)

As participants arrive, welcome them to the study and invite them to make use of one of the available Bibles, if they did not bring one. Offer the following prayer, pray one of your own, or invite a group member to pray.

Fill us with your love, O God. Help us to see, to hear, to feel, and to offer your grace in all that we share this day. Amen.

Video (15 minutes)

Play the video for Session 4. The segment suggests that lasting happiness is a way of being, not simply a feeling or a state of mind. Miofsky challenges us to live into the life God desires for us rather than chasing our own desires. Happiness is a way of being that is in tune with what God wants for us.

Choose from the following for a brief discussion:

- Miofsky says, "Happiness is the life that is truly life." What does he mean by that? What does that statement mean to you?

- Some would argue that happiness comes from a greater focus on the self. Do you agree with this? Why or why not? How can a focus on others lead to greater happiness?

Biblical Foundation (5 minutes)

Invite a volunteer to read Luke 9:23-34 out loud. Reflect on the contradictions contained in Jesus' words: "all who want to save their lives will lose them... all who lose their lives because of me will save them" (9:24).

Jesus' crucifixion is given here as an example of the kind of sacrifice one is called to make in order to follow Christ. When he says that "all who want to save their lives will lose them," he is referring to those who have left their homes, families, and jobs, as well as those who have given away all their possessions or even died for Christ.

- What do you think Jesus meant by these statements? How do these verses relate to lasting happiness?

- What do these words mean for your own relationship with Christ?

Book Study (20 minutes)

Visualize Your Own Awesomeness

Distribute sheets of paper and crayons to each member of the group. Consider together the author's "suggestions" for finding happiness: writing down achievements, making yourself a priority, filling your day with things you love, and creating visuals of your own awesomeness. Think about that last one. Even though Miofsky warns that this is not the key to lasting happiness, have the group create visuals of their own awesomeness just to see where this activity leads.

When the group is finished drawing, have those who are willing share their pictures (which will surely be humorous). Discuss whether the things depicted are sources of happiness. Does God's desire appear anywhere? What about acts of generosity? Does what makes a person "awesome" actually make a person happy? How do the good things you visualize about yourself illustrate the role you can play in God's work?

Feeling Generous

The author writes, "As tempted as we may be to hoard what we have, these scientific studies seem to indicate that we are indeed hardwired to give." Divide the class into two groups. Have one group develop an argument that giving does *not* come naturally to human beings; instead, they are predisposed to self-interest. What evidence would support this claim? Does it have any scriptural warrant? Ask the second group to develop the author's argument that people are hardwired to give. What evidence does he present to support this? What examples would you cite to make this claim?

Optional Activity (up to 30 minutes extra)

Epiphany

Miofsky opens with a story from school when he faced a difficult math problem he wasn't able to solve with any amount of work. Finally, when he turned his attention away from the problem, the answer leapt to his mind. This also happens, he says, with happiness. The more we focus on our own happiness, the less likely we are to experience it. It is only when we focus on something or someone else that lasting happiness takes hold.

Ask the group to consider this story. Take five minutes for individual reflection and think about a time when the answer or feeling came to you just when you shifted your mind away from the problem. Can you think of examples where this has happened with happiness? How can focusing on someone or something else bring the kind of deep contentment the author describes?

Journaling the Week Ahead (5 minutes)

At this point in the session, distribute Session 4 Handout with journal prompts and additional questions. Explain to the class that the handout is for their personal use in the week ahead to continue to explore the issues raised in class.

Closing Prayer (2 minutes)

God of grace, joy, and hope, God of loving relationship, walk with us as we see with new eyes, hear with new ears, as we build our lives on the essentials of faith. Amen.

JOURNALING THE WEEK AHEAD

In John 10:10, Jesus says, "The thief enters only to steal, kill, and destroy. I came so that they could have life—indeed, so that they could live life to the fullest." How do you interpret the phrase "live life to the fullest"? In what way does your relationship with Jesus help you to live life to the fullest?

_____

_____

_____

_____

_____

_____

Does focusing on others mean we can never pursue the things we enjoy? Can people with jobs, homes, and families really put Jesus first and "lose their lives"?

_____

_____

_____

_____

_____

What are some signs that God is pushing you to be vulnerable and share your story? Think of the example the author offers of his alcoholic friend. How did the friend know that God wanted to use his story to affect other people? Have you ever had this experience?

_____

_____

_____

_____

_____

_____

The author emphasizes the importance of a change in perspective for achieving lasting happiness. How can generosity help accomplish a change in perspective? Have you ever had the experience of generosity making you happy?

_____

_____

_____

_____

_____

_____

_____

CPSIA information can be obtained
at www.ICGtesting.com
Printed in the USA
LVOW13s0349210217
524865LV00001B/2/P